NOW THAT I BELIEVE

D0282368

NOW THAT I BELIEVE

ROBERT A. COOK

MOODY PUBLISHERS
CHICAGO

ISBN: 0-8024-5983-8
ISBN-13: 978-0-8024-5983-1

We hope you enjoy this book from Moody Publishers. Our goal is to provide high-quality, thought-provoking books and products that connect truth to your real needs and challenges. For more information on other books and products written and produced from a biblical perspective, go to www.moodypublishers.com or write to:

Moody Publishers
820 N. LaSalle Boulevard
Chicago, IL 60610

123 125 127 129 130 128 126 124

Printed in the United States of America

INTRODUCTION

Anything from the pen of Dr. Robert Cook is not only very good reading but it is important. *Now That I Believe*, written for young people, has grown out of his own experience of salvation. It is biblical, dynamic, and soul-stirring.

Now That I Believe is not optional. It is a MUST for every young man and young woman who wants to make progress and be victorious in the Christian life. We recommend this volume as being most profitable for widespread distribution, especially among Christian young people.

DR. TORREY M. JOHNSON

*　　*　　*　　*　　*

Medical and scientific resources are constantly being employed and increased to combat the rather high mortality rate among children in their first year of life, due to the diseases peculiar to that period. It is not what it was years ago, but it is still high.

It seems to me that the spiritual mortality rate among "babes in Christ" is high, if we are to judge by the growth of our evangelical churches and the extension of our home and foreign missionary effort. The reasons for it and the opinions expressed about it may be legion, but I believe that the use of this book by pastors and Christian workers dealing with young Christians will result in a diminishing number of confused, frustrated, backsliding, emaciated beginners in the Christian life and an increase in spiritual stalwarts. To this end, I recommend the extensive use of this book.

CEDRIC SEARS

THIS BOOK . . .

. . . presupposes the new birth. Of course it is impossible to live the Christian life until one has started that existence—been born again. Remind yourself right now that the supreme value in this world is to be right with God through faith in Jesus Christ. If there is any doubt whatever about that relationship, get down on your knees, confess your sins, and receive the Lord Jesus, by faith, into your life.

"But as many as received Him, to them He gave the right to become the children of God, even to those who believe in His name" (John 1:12). For immediate, thoughtful consideration of the Scripture used in this book, and only where the small reference numeral is used, we refer you to the closing portion of each chapter.

CONTENTS

I walk in a daze and yet am conscious. I know myself to be a citizen of another world but live familiarly in this one. I sense a change in my desires, convictions, beliefs—but am still the same personality. I love my friends and long for their salvation but am strangely out of step with their pagan way of life. I weep where once I laughed and laugh where once I wept. I am tender where once I was ruthless, yet unyielding where once I gave way to pressures and temptations. I am a new person, yet the same person. . . . What happened to me?

1

WHAT HAPPENED TO ME?

A MIRACLE

You, my friend, are a direct proof of the statement that the age of miracles is not past. For you, yourself, are a miracle. God's description of a Christian indicates that fact most clearly: "Therefore, if anyone is in Christ, he is a new creation, old things have passed away; behold, all things have become new" (2 Corinthians 5:17).

Our Lord Jesus made this truth His basic approach to one of the most learned men in His day—Nicodemus.[1]

"Nicodemus," He said, "you must be born again. If not, you'll never see the kingdom of God."

Nicodemus raised an immediate objection.

"How can these things be?" Perplexity, the result of an unsaved heart trying to analyze salvation, was in his voice.

Our Lord answered patiently, tenderly. "Nicodemus," He said, "do not marvel that I said to you 'You must be born again.' You can't explain it—true. But you can't explain a lot of other things, either. Take the wind, for instance. Can you tell where it came from, and where it is going? No. You can feel it, hear it whispering through the leaves, but you can't explain it. Neither can you explain salvation.

"Here's the difficulty," He continued. "You were born once, with an earthly nature. You're a sinner, Nicodemus, and you have a sinful nature. That which is born of the flesh is flesh and nothing more! How do you ever expect to get past the judgment of a holy God with nothing but sinful flesh? You have to have another birth, Nicodemus, a birth from above. Let's call it a birth of the Spirit, because He's the One who is active in it. When *that* occurs, you'll have a new, holy nature, for that which is born of the Spirit is spirit."

Essentially, salvation is the miracle of receiving life. There is nothing so hopelessly still as a corpse. No scientist has yet been able to breathe life into a dead body. Just as hopeless is the sinner without Christ. He is "dead in trespasses and sins."[2] Nor has he any prospect of doing better, for "those who are in the flesh cannot please God" (Romans 8:8).

Our Lord Jesus emphasized this truth when

He said: "It is the Spirit who gives life; the flesh profits nothing. The words that I speak to you are spirit, and they are life" (John 6:63). And "he who hears My word and believes in Him who sent Me has everlasting life, and shall not come into judgment, but has passed from death into life" (John 5:24).

Yes, a miracle happened to you when you were saved. The Lord Jesus touched your life with His nail-scarred hand and gave you new life, with a new nature—*His* life, and *His* nature!

YOU MET A WONDERFUL PERSON

Salvation is not something you do, but something Christ does when you receive Him. "But as many as received Him, to them He gave the right to become children of God, even to those who believe in His name" (John 1:12). Personal testimonies in the gospels and the Acts highlight this fact.

Andrew, talking to Simon Peter: " 'We have found the Messiah' (which is translated, the Christ). And he brought him to Jesus" (John 1:41).

Philip, to Nathanael: "We have found Him of whom Moses in the law, and also the prophets, wrote—Jesus of Nazareth, the son of Joseph" (John 1:45).

The woman of Samaria: "Come, see a Man who told me all things that I ever did. Could this be the Christ?" (John 4:29).

Paul, before Agrippa: "At midday, O king, I saw a light, and I heard a voice and I said, 'Who are You, Lord?' And He said, 'I am Jesus, whom you are persecuting. But rise and stand on your feet; for I have appeared to you for this purpose, to make you a minister and a witness both of the things which you have seen and of the things which I will yet reveal to you.' "[3]

It is easy to see why this personal emphasis must be. *Only a person could reveal God to me:* "He who came down from heaven[4] . . . The only begotten Son, who is in the bosom of the Father, He has declared Him."[5] *Only a person could meet my personal need and heal sin's deadly sting:* "And as Moses lifted up the serpent in the wilderness, even so must the Son of Man be lifted up, that whoever believes in Him should not perish but have eternal life" (John 3:14-15). *Only a person—a divine Person—could bestow everlasting life:* "For God so loved the world that He gave His only begotten Son, that whoever believes in Him should not perish but have everlasting life" (John 3:16). And *it takes a person to satisfy and keep me:* "You are complete in Him[6] . . . For all things are yours: whether Paul or Apollos or Cephas, or the world or life or death, or things present or things to come—

14

all are yours. And you are Christ's, and Christ is God's" (1 Corinthians 3:21-23). When I approach God, I am accepted "in the Beloved"[7]— *a Person*—and my daily goal is to "be found *in Him*, not having my own righteousness, which is from the law, but that which is through the faith of Christ, the righteousness which is from God by faith" (Philippians 3:9).

Salvation is not something—it's Somebody! When you were saved, you met a Person, you opened your life to Him, and you are now living under His control. Paul said: "I know whom I have believed and am persuaded that He is able to keep what I have committed to Him until that Day."[8]

YOU BECAME PART OF AN ETERNAL TRANSACTION

"For what does the Scripture say? 'Abraham believed God, and it was accounted to him for righteousness.' Now to him who works, the wages are not counted as grace but as debt. But to him who does not work but believes on Him who justifies the ungodly, *his faith is accounted for righteousness*" (Romans 4:3-5).

Let us get the picture straight. What does God demand? Righteousness.

What can I offer? Only sin and more sin.[9]

Can I ever hope to do better under my own

power? No, because I am condemned already without Christ.[10]

How may I obtain the righteousness that God demands? Simply by receiving it by faith.[11]

When I receive Christ, does that alter my standing before God? Certainly it does. God takes the righteousness of Christ and puts it to my account. Because Jesus died for me, God can both "be just and the justifier of the one who has faith in Jesus" (Romans 3:26).

Someone says, "I still don't understand it."

Look then at this verse: "God was in Christ reconciling the world to Himself, not imputing their trespasses to them. . . . For He made Him who knew no sin to be sin for us, that we might become the righteousness of God in Him."[12] Who was sinned against? God.

Who alone could settle the score of sin? God.

Who was it, suffering on the cross for sin? God.

Has the debt been paid? Yes, because "the Lord has laid on Him the iniquity of us all,"[13] and He "Himself bore our sins in His own body on the tree, that we, having died to sins, might live for righteousness—by whose stripes you were healed" (1 Peter 2:24).

If *God* is the one sinned against and *God* has paid the debt and settled the score, does *God* have a right to give to me, freely, His righteousness? Yes, hallelujah! It is free: "even the righteousness of God which is through faith in Jesus Christ to all and on all who believe. . . . being justified freely by His grace through the redemption that is in Christ Jesus" (Romans 3:22, 24).

Here, then, is the transaction that takes place at conversion: God forgives my sin,[14] imputes and imparts His righteousness,[15] makes me forever His child,[16] and gives me an inheritance with Christ.[17] *He* does it, mind you, not I. No wonder we shout, Hallelujah, what a Savior!

This is what happened to you. You experienced a miracle: you met a Person, and you became part of an eternal transaction.

Every part of this truth is initiated by, and dependent upon, Almighty God. If He started it, He certainly will finish it. All of which brings us to a discussion of the unspoken fear of every new convert: What if my Christian joy should not last? Turn to chapter 2, and see what God's Word says on the subject.

COORDINATE SCRIPTURE FOR CHAPTER 1

1. There was a man of the Pharisees, named Nicodemus, a ruler of the Jews. This man came to Jesus by night and said to Him, "Rabbi, we know that You

17

are a teacher come from God; for no one can do these signs that You do unless God is with him."

Jesus answered and said to him, "Most assuredly, I say to you, unless one is born again, he cannot see the kingdom of God."

Nicodemus said to Him, "How can a man be born when he is old? Can he enter the second time into his mother's womb and be born?"

Jesus answered, "Most assuredly, I say to you, unless one is born of water and the Spirit, he cannot enter the kingdom of God.

"That which is born of the flesh is flesh, and that which is born of the Spirit is spirit. Do not marvel that I said to you, 'You must be born again.' The wind blows where it wishes, and you hear the sound of it, but cannot tell where it comes from and where it goes. So is everyone who is born of the Spirit."

Nicodemus answered and said to Him, "How can these things be?"

Jesus answered and said to him, "Are you the teacher of Israel, and do not know these things? Most assuredly, I say to you, We speak what We know and testify what We have seen, and you do not receive Our witness.

"If I have told you earthly things and you do not believe, how will you believe if I tell you heavenly things?

"No one has ascended to heaven but He who came down from heaven, that is, the Son of Man who is in heaven.

"And as Moses lifted up the serpent in the wilderness, even so must the Son of Man be lifted up, that whosoever believes in Him should not perish but have eternal life. For God so loved the world that He gave His only begotten Son, that whoever believes in Him should not perish but have everlasting life" (John 3:1-16).

2. And you He made alive, who were dead in trespasses and sins (Ephesians 2:1).

3. "While thus occupied, as I journeyed to Damascus with authority and commission from the chief priests, at midday, O king, along the road I saw a light from heaven, brighter than the sun, shining around me and those who journeyed with me.

"And when we all had fallen to the ground, I heard a voice speaking to me and saying in the Hebrew language, 'Saul, Saul, why are you persecuting Me? It is hard for you to kick against the goads.'

"So I said, 'Who are You, Lord?' And He said, 'I am Jesus, whom you are persecuting.

'But rise and stand on your feet; for I have appeared to you for this purpose, to make you a minister and a witness both of the things which you have seen and of the things which I will yet reveal to you.

'I will deliver you from the Jewish people, as well as from the Gentiles, to whom I now send you,

'to open their eyes, and to turn them from darkness to light, and from the power of Satan to God, that they may receive forgiveness of sins and an inheritance among those who are sanctified by faith in Me.'

"Therefore, King Agrippa, I was not disobedient to the heavenly vision, but declared first to those in Damascus and in Jerusalem, and throughout all the region of Judea, and then to the Gentiles, that they should repent, turn to God, and do works befitting repentance" (Acts 26:12-20).

4. No one has ascended to heaven but He who came down from heaven, that is, the Son of Man who is in heaven (John 3:13).

5. No one has seen God at any time. The only begotten Son, who is in the bosom of the Father, He has declared Him (John 1:18).

6. And you are complete in Him, who is the head of all principality and power (Colossians 2:10).

7. To the praise of the glory of His grace, by which He has made us accepted in the Beloved (Ephesians 1:6).

8. For this reason I also suffer these things; nevertheless I am not ashamed, for I know whom I have believed, and am persuaded that He is able to keep what I have committed to Him until that Day (2 Timothy 1:12).

9. As it is written: "There is none righteous, no, not one; there is none who understands; there is none who seeks after God. They have all gone out of the way; They have together become unprofitable; There is none who does good, no, not one.

"Their throat is an open tomb; With their tongues

they have practiced deceit; The poison of asps *is* under their lips;

"Whose mouth is full of cursing and bitterness.

"Their feet are swift to shed blood;

Destruction and misery are in their ways;

And the way of peace they have not known.

"There is no fear of God before their eyes."

Now we know that whatever the law says, it says to those who are under the law, that every mouth may be stopped, and all the world may become guilty before God.

Therefore by the deeds of the law no flesh will be justified in His sight, for by the law is the knowledge of sin (Romans 3:10-20).

10. He who believes in Him is not condemned; but he who does not believe is condemned already, because he has not believed in the name of the only begotten Son of God (John 3:18).

11. Even the righteousness of God which is through faith in Jesus Christ to all and on all who believe. For there is no difference (Romans 3:22).

12. That is, that God was in Christ reconciling the world to Himself, not imputing their trespasses to them, and has committed to us the word of reconciliation.

Therefore, we are ambassadors for Christ, as though God were pleading through us: we implore you on Christ's behalf, be reconciled to God.

For He made Him who knew no sin to be sin for us, that we might become the righteousness of God in Him (2 Corinthians 5:19-21).

13. All we like sheep have gone astray; We have turned, every one, to his own way; And the Lord has laid on Him the iniquity of us all (Isaiah 53:6).

14. And you, being dead in your trespasses and the uncircumcision of your flesh, He has made alive together with Him, having forgiven you all trespasses (Colossians 2:13).

15. Even the righteousness of God which is through faith in Jesus Christ to all and on all who believe. For there is no difference (Romans 3:22).

16. But as many as received Him, to them He gave the right to become children of God, even to those who believe in His name (John 1:12).

17. The Spirit Himself bears witness with our spirit that we are children of God, and if children, then heirs—heirs of God and joint heirs with Christ, if indeed we suffer with Him, that we may also be glorified together (Romans 8:16-17).

For the first time in my life, I know joy. Happiness I have had . . . fleeting enjoyment based on things, and circumstances, and people. I have learned by experience that the pleasures of sin "are but for a season." And I have known the staleness of surfeit, the acrid taste of disappointment, the bitterness of regret, the utterly unsatisfying nature of all things earthy. Now I have joy—the pure delight of a soul that is right with God. What if . . . what if something should destroy that relation? What if I fail? What if the joy does not last?

2

HOW LONG WILL THIS NEW-FOUND JOY LAST?

Your joy is not an end in itself, but a result. It comes from the fact that you are in a right relationship to God through faith in Christ.

Even this relationship is not an end in itself. It stems in turn from the eternal purposes of God Almighty. "Known to God from eternity are all His works" (Acts 15:18). Paul speaks of Christians as those who are "called according to His purpose."[1] Christians were chosen in Christ "before the foundation of the world."[2]

You thought your Christian life started when you knelt at Calvary, and so it did. But at the same time, you stepped into the mighty current of the purpose of God, and all that you are today depends upon your relation to that eternal plan.

It is necessary that you see this truth clearly. Humanly, we tend to think of ourselves as being quite important. Prove this by asking yourself whose picture you look for *first* in any group photo! God's point of view is entirely different. When we stand at the cross and look at life with Him, we are not nearly so important as we thought. Rather, His will . . . His plan . . . His purpose become the main issues of our lives.

"Very well," you say. "I know that my joy comes *from* God. But that is not my trouble. Now, what if I should lose it? Then what?"

Before you worry further, turn to the Word. "According to the eternal purpose which He accomplished in Christ Jesus our Lord" (Ephesians 3:11).

What kind of purpose is it of which you are a part?

An *eternal* purpose.

How long is an eternal purpose?

Forever and ever.

Is that long enough to see me through this life and get me to heaven? If it is, then what am I worrying about?

This is the sense of that blessed promise in Philippians: "Being confident of this very thing, that He who has begun a good work in you will complete it until the day of Jesus Christ" (1:6).

If God planned it, initiated it, saw it to fruition in my soul, tied His almightiness and His heavenly reputation to it, then certainly I ought to trust Him with the working out of His eternal purpose.

Many a failure in the Christian life originates right here. People often come to me and say, "I'm through . . . I've failed . . . I can't keep up the Christian life." Frequently I'll answer them, "Well, praise God."

Shocked they will ask, "What is there to praise God about?"

Simply, the answer is this: Thank God you've discovered that you cannot produce nor maintain the Christian life. God must do it, or it simply isn't done! More about this later.

How long will my joy last? As long as God is God and His Word is truth . . . as long as the eternal purpose of God is operative in the universe . . . forever! The Lord Jesus meant what He said when He remarked, "And I give them eternal life, and they shall never perish."[3]

Another lesson we must learn is that the lasting quality of salvation is quite apart from circumstances. Peter wrote to people who were going through trials: "You greatly rejoice, though now for a little while, if need be, you have been grieved by various trials . . . that the genuineness of your faith . . . may be found to praise, honor, and glory at the revelation of Jesus Christ, whom having not seen you love. Though now you do not see Him, yet believing, you rejoice with joy inexpressible and full of glory."[4]

Happiness depends upon what happens—circumstances. When circumstances are adverse, I am unhappy. When they are favorable, I am happy.

Joy, however, according to this passage, can be had when circumstances are completely in reverse. Look at the circumstances and you get "grieved . . . various trials . . . genuineness of your faith." Look at Jesus, and you get "greatly rejoice . . . rejoice with joy inexpressible and full of glory!" Your joy is a Person and will last as long as that Person lasts!

Furthermore, joy in Christ can make even unhappy circumstances serve you . . . work for your good. This is exactly what Paul says: "For our light affliction, which is but for a moment, is working for us a far more exceeding and eternal weight of glory" (2 Corinthians 4:17).

"Working for us"—what works for me? Affliction—the very thing that had me scared . . . threatened to make me quit! God is making my enemy work for me!

The same truth is expressed in Romans 5 where Paul says: "We also glory in tribulations, knowing that tribulation produces perseverance; and perseverance, character; and character, hope. Now hope does not disappoint."[5]

Go a step farther and look at Romans 8:28:

"And we know that all things work together for good to those who love God, to those who are the called according to His purpose." There's the glorious truth: Since you belong to Jesus Christ, and since your life now operates under His sovereignty, nothing can touch your life without working *for* you, producing good!

Do you dare to worry when you know Almighty God is concerning Himself about your every experience?

SUBSISTENCE—OR GROWTH?

Everything depends upon where you place the emphasis in this matter. Inevitably, if you seek merely to maintain what you now have— hoard it, keep it, preserve it—you are going to be disappointed. Any businessman knows that when he comes to the place where he is only holding on to the clients he has and not getting any new business, he's through. So it is in the Christian life. Peter says: "As newborn babes, desire the pure milk of the word, that you may grow thereby" (1 Peter 2:2). And "grow in the grace and knowledge of our Lord and Savior Jesus Christ."[6] Paul remarked to the Thessalonians that "your faith grows exceedingly."[7] He also besought them to "increase more and more."[8] And the Lord Jesus said to His disciples: "These things I have spoken to you, that

My joy may remain in you, and that your joy may be full . . . these things I speak in the world, that they may have My joy fulfilled in themselves."[9]

Put the emphasis where it belongs! Don't try to "hold on" to Christian joy. Go on with Christ in the Word, and joy will take care of itself—you'll be full of joy because you're filled with *Him!*

Here is the heart of the matter: You're part of an eternal purpose . . . you're linked with an eternally lovely Person . . . you're experiencing a lifelong process of growth in His grace.

Salvation is not something to be endured. Enjoy it, friend, enjoy it!

COORDINATE SCRIPTURE FOR
CHAPTER 2

1. And we know that all things work together for good to those who love God, to those who are the called according to His purpose (Romans 8:28).

2. Just as He chose us in Him before the foundation of the world, that we should be holy and without blame before Him in love (Ephesians 1:4).

3. And I give them eternal life, and they shall never perish; neither shall anyone snatch them out of My hand (John 10:28).

4. In this you greatly rejoice, though now for a little while, if need be, you have been grieved by various trials, that the genuineness of your faith, being much more precious than gold that perishes, though it is tested by fire, may be found to praise, honor, and glory at the revelation of Jesus Christ, whom having not seen you love. Though now you do not see Him, yet believing, you rejoice with joy inexpressible and full of glory (1 Peter 1:6-8).

5. And not only that, but we also glory in tribulations, knowing that tribulation produces perseverance; and perseverance, character; and character, hope.

Now hope does not disappoint, because the love of God has been poured out in our hearts by the Holy Spirit who was given to us (Romans 5:3-5).

6. But grow in the grace and knowledge of our Lord and Savior Jesus Christ. To Him be the glory both now and forever. Amen (2 Peter 3:18).

7. We are bound to thank God always for you, brethren, as it is fitting, because your faith grows exceedingly, and the love of every one of you all abounds toward each other (2 Thessalonians 1:3).

8. And indeed you do so toward all the brethren who are in all Macedonia. But we urge you, brethren, that you increase more and more (1 Thessalonians 4:10).

9. But now I come to You, and these things I speak in the world, that they may have My joy fulfilled in themselves (John 17:13).

Well, I've started . . . wonder how long I can hold out. Folks claim it will "wear off," as they say. That makes religion sound like a hangover! I certainly know that there are some stiff battles up ahead. I've got to make the grade somehow . . . nothing worse than to make this profession and then have to come crawling back to the old crowd to admit that I'm licked. I'll try—but is trying enough?

3

THE BATTLE AHEAD
or
What to Do in Temptation

The first thing to do about temptation is to expect it. There is nothing unusual or abnormal about being tempted. Rather, the person who is never tempted should question whether he is spiritually alive!

Let us get the proper approach to this matter. Not, "Why must I be tempted . . . go through all this testing?" Rather, "People *are* tempted; that much I know. I am not any different from other human beings, therefore I shall be tempted. What provision does God make for me?"

The Bible takes temptation for granted. Our Lord Jesus was "in all points tempted as we are."[1] He felt the mental anguish that temptation occasions, too, for we read, "He Himself has suffered, being tempted."[2]

James says that, rather than being thrown into a panic by it, we are to "count it all joy when you fall into various trials" (James 1:2), and Peter assures us that "the Lord knows how to deliver the godly out of temptations."[3] Paul remarks that your temptation is no different from the testing to which everyone else is subjected—"such as is common to man,"[4] and the Lord Jesus Christ teaches us as His disciples to pray, "Do not lead us into temptation."[5]

The devil's business is temptation. He tempted the Lord Jesus—in fact, he is called the tempter in Matthew 4:3, and Paul calls Satan the tempter in writing to the Thessalonians.[6] Do you think the devil is going out of business just because you were converted?

Learn to recognize temptation when it comes. James says that temptation is based upon desire: "Each one is tempted when he is drawn away by his own desires and enticed" (James 1:14).

Every one of us has certain natural desires— God made us that way. We desire food, fellowship, self-preservation, a sense of accomplishment—many other things. Then, because we are members of a sinful race, we have certain wrong desires—to cheat, and lie, and be avenged, and get the better of our fellowman. These good and evil desires are mixed together in the chemistry of your soul. Satan operates on the basis of using *what you already want* as a means of leading you into sin.

Of course it is simple enough to recognize

temptation based upon wrong desires. If it's a wrong desire, it will lead to a wrong act, and you know it. Never act upon a wrong desire— you will only get into more sin and trouble.

Not so easily identified, however, are temptations based upon good and legitimate desires. Remember at the very outset that Satan is interested in taking that which is good in your life and prostituting it to his own devilish ends. Here are a couple of questions that will help you settle the matter.

I am about to take this or that course of action. Does it glorify God?[7] Can I do it in the name of the Lord Jesus and offer a prayer of thanksgiving over it?[8] Does it make me more preoccupied with "things," or does it help me in spending more time at the feet of Jesus?[9] Does it help to build up (edify) my Christian life, or does it tear down?[10] Will it offend another?[11]

If you will honestly ask these questions regarding any doubtful course of action, you will recognize temptation when it comes and will be prepared to resist it in the power that Christ gives.

Having recognized temptation, the next thing is to resist it. Let us be honest about this business. The Christian faith is not an automatic cure-all for you. If you *want* to go on in sin you *will* go on in sin, and nothing can stop you! Unless you want to be different, you never will be different. And until you desire victory over temptation enough to take a stand against it, you'll get exactly nowhere.

Search your heart today, remembering that it is "deceitful above all things, and desperately wicked,"[12] and find out the truth. Do I want victory over temptation and sin, or do I want an easy way to forgiveness and heaven *while remaining in sin?*

Basically, taking your stand toward temptation is taking your stand with Christ. This is nothing new, because you did it when you came for salvation. You said, "When Christ died, I died *with* Him, because He was dying *for* me. When He rose, I rose *with* Him. Therefore, I trust Him as my Savior and identify myself with Him for salvation."[13] Now, as you face temptation, identify yourself afresh with your blessed Lord. Does He hate sin? Then so must you! Does He desire holiness of character and life? Then let that desire be fanned into flame in your soul. Gladden God's heart with a response like that of the little child. Seated at a restaurant table, faced with a choice from among a dozen possible items, she said simply, "Papa, I want what *you* want." "And because you are sons, God has sent forth the Spirit of His Son into your hearts, crying out, 'Abba, Father!' " (Gal. 4:6).

Granted now that you are prepared to resist

temptation because of being identified with Christ, never make the mistake of attempting it in your own strength. You started with Him—He did the saving work that made you a child of God. Don't leave Him now and flounder about trying to keep yourself afloat. Well does Paul ask, "Having begun in the Spirit, are you now being made perfect by the flesh?" No, he says, "The just shall *live* by faith."[14] You started by faith—simply trusting Jesus. Now keep right on the same way!

See what the Word says about God, and temptation, and you. He knows how to deliver the godly out of temptation.[15] He knows how you feel, because He suffered, being tempted.[16] He will never allow you to be tested beyond your power to endure.[17] He encourages you to watch and pray that you enter not into temptation.[18] And He promises to keep you.[19]

Even more specifically, the business of the Lord Jesus Christ is to represent you—and your need—to God the Father. "Therefore He is also able to save to the uttermost those who come to God through Him, since He ever lives to make intercession for them" (Hebrews 7:25).

He is able—because He is God.

To save—because He died for me.

To the uttermost—there will never be a situation, never a temptation, that He cannot handle.

He ever lives to make intercession for them—day and night, the wounded hands of Jesus are stretched forth to God the Father in eloquent pleading . . . not only to save me, but to keep me as well!

We left out one phrase in the above breakdown. What was it? "Those . . . who come to God through Him." What kind of persons does the Lord Jesus help in temptation? Those that come to God and ask for help through Him! God will never do the coming and the asking *for* you. Jesus died for you and now lives for you, but you must come for yourself.

If you are determined to resist temptation in the strength that God gives, come to the throne of grace and receive it! "Let us therefore come boldly to the throne of grace, that we may obtain mercy and find grace to help in time of need" (Heb. 4:16).

You should call for help NOW, when you need help. Too many times we make the mistake of postponing our praying. Later, too late, we pray sadly, "Lord, I failed. Please forgive and cleanse me." Now such praying is effective, and we shall speak of it in a moment, but is it not infinitely better to pray *now,* when I need help, and receive it? Our verse speaks of help "in time of need." Actually, this means "in the nick o'time."

> Just when I need Him most,
> Just when I need Him most;
> Jesus is near to comfort and cheer,
> Just when I need Him most!

It is important to recognize the place of the Word of God in helping you to meet temptation. You may be absolutely certain of this: The only thing you are *naturally* capable of is sin and more sin, failure and more failure. Only the Word of God taking root in your life can change the natural into the supernatural. "How can a young man cleanse his way? By taking heed according to Your word. . . . Your word I have hidden in my heart, That I might not sin against you" (Ps. 119:9, 11). Paul speaks of "the washing of water by the word,"[20] and the Lord Jesus said, "You are already clean because of the word which I have spoken to you" (John 15:3).

Christ used the Word of God exclusively in dealing with Satan during the wilderness temptation.[21] To every leering suggestion of the devil, our blessed Lord answered, "It is written . . ." After the final, triumphant Scripture, "It is written, you shall worship the Lord your God, and Him only shall you serve," we read, "Then the devil left Him." Hallelujah!

There is a Scripture answer to every suggestion Satan can ever make. Know the Word, and you'll know the sweet taste of victory over temptation.

Habit is important in dealing with temptation. Monotonously, you kept on failing before . . . now form the habit of bringing everything to Jesus and make victory as habitual as failure ever was! Not by chance does the old song say,

> Each victory will help you
> Some other to win.

What if you fail? You are still quite capable of failure. Should it occur, confess your sin immediately, being explicit about it in prayer. The "Lord bless me" kind of prayer will not do here. It's "Lord, I lied," or "I cheated," or whatever may have occurred. "If we confess our sins, He is faithful and just to forgive us our sins and to cleanse us from all unrighteousness" (1 John 1:9).

Never let a day go by but that you are, as the old-timers used to say, "confessed and prayed up to date." That is what the Word of God calls "walking in the light." And "if we walk in the light as He is in the light, we have fellowship one with one another, and the blood of Jesus Christ His Son cleanses us from all sin" (1 John 1:7).

You are ready now to deal with temptation.

Expect it, recognize it, resist it, depend on God only, and use the Word.

COORDINATE SCRIPTURE FOR CHAPTER 3

1. For we do not have a High Priest who cannot sympathize with our weaknesses, but was in all points tempted as we are, yet without sin (Hebrews 4:15).

2. For in that He Himself has suffered, being tempted, He is able to aid those who are tempted (Hebrews 2:18).

3. The Lord knows how to deliver the godly out of temptations and to reserve the unjust under punishment for the day of judgment (2 Peter 2:9).

4. No temptation has overtaken you except such as is common to man; but God is faithful, who will not allow you to be tempted beyond what you are able, but with the temptation will also make the way of escape, that you may be able to bear it (1 Corinthians 10:13).

5. And do not lead us into temptation, But deliver us from the evil one. For Yours is the kingdom and the power and the glory forever. Amen (Matthew 6:13).

6. For this reason, when I could no longer endure it, I sent to know your faith, lest by some means the

tempter had tempted you, and our labor might be in vain (1 Thessalonians 3:5).

7. Therefore, whether you eat or drink, or whatever you do, do all to the glory of God (1 Corinthians 10:31).

8. And whatever you do in word or deed, do all in the name of the Lord Jesus, giving thanks to God the Father through Him (Colossians 3:17).

9. And the cares of this world, the deceitfulness of riches, and the desires for other things entering in choke the word, and it becomes unfruitful (Mark 4:19).

And Jesus answered and said to her, "Martha, Martha, you are worried and troubled about many things" (Luke 10:41).

10. How is it then, brethren? Whenever you come together, each of you has a psalm, has a teaching, has a tongue, has a revelation, has an interpretation. Let all things be done for edification.

All things are lawful for me, but all things are not helpful; all things are lawful for me, but all things do not edify (1 Corinthians 14:26; 10:23).

11. And because of your knowledge shall the weak brother perish, for whom Christ died?

But when you thus sin against the brethren, and wound their weak conscience, you sin against Christ.

Therefore, if food makes my brother stumble, I will never again eat meat, lest I make my brother stumble (1 Corinthians 8:11-13).

12. The heart is deceitful above all things. And desperately wicked; Who can know it (Jeremiah 17:9)?

13. I have been crucified with Christ; it is no longer I who live, but Christ lives in me; and the life which I now live in the flesh I live by faith in the Son of God, who loved me and gave Himself for me (Galatians 2:20).

Therefore we were buried with Him through baptism into death, that just as Christ was raised from the dead by the glory of the Father, even so we also should walk in newness of life.

For if we have been united together in the likeness of His death, certainly we also shall be in the likeness of His resurrection (Romans 6:4-5).

14. Are you so foolish? Having begun in the Spirit, are you now being made perfect by the flesh?

But that no one is justified by the law in the sight of God is evident, for "The just shall live by faith" (Galatians 3:3, 11).

15. The Lord knows how to deliver the godly out of temptations and to reserve the unjust under punishment for the day of judgment (2 Peter 2:9).

16. For in that He Himself has suffered, being tempted, He is able to aid those who are tempted (Hebrews 2:18).

17. No temptation has overtaken you except such as is common to man; but God is faithful, who will not allow you to be tempted beyond what you are able, but with the temptation will also make a way of

escape, that you may be able to bear it (1 Corinthians 10:13).

18. Watch and pray, lest you enter into temptation. The spirit indeed is willing, but the flesh is weak (Matthew 26:41).

19. Because you have kept My command to persevere, I also will keep you from the hour of trial which shall come upon the whole world, to test those who dwell on the earth (Revelation 3:10).

To an inheritance incorruptible and undefiled and that does not fade away, reserved in heaven for you, who are kept by the power of God through faith for salvation ready to be revealed in the last time.

In this you greatly rejoice, though now for a little while, if need be, you have been grieved by various trials (1 Peter 1:4-6).

20. That He might sanctify and cleanse it with the washing of water by the word (Ephesians 5:26).

21. Then Jesus was led up by the Spirit into the wilderness to be tempted by the devil. And when He had fasted forty days and forty nights, afterward He was hungry.

Now when the tempter came to Him, he said, "If You are the Son of God, command that these stones become bread." But He answered and said, "It is written, 'Man shall not live by bread alone, but by every word that proceeds from the mouth of God.' "

Then the devil took Him up into the holy city, set Him on the pinnacle of the temple, and said to Him, "If You are the Son of God, throw Yourself down.

For it is written: 'He shall give His angels charge concerning you,' and, 'In their hands they shall bear you up, Lest you dash your foot against a stone.' "

Jesus said to him, "It is written again, 'You shall not tempt the Lord your God.' "

Again, the devil took Him up on an exceedingly high mountain, and showed Him all the kingdoms of the world and their glory.

And he said to Him, "All these things I will give You if You will fall down and worship me."

Then Jesus said to him, "Away with you, Satan! For it is written, 'You shall worship the Lord your God, and Him only you shall serve.' "

Then the devil left Him, and behold, angels came and ministered to Him (Matthew 4:1-11).

People confuse me . . . some say, "Do," others, "Don't." Some have extremely high standards and are utterly devoted to Christ, while others are not so strict, but seem to love the Lord just as much. After whom do I pattern . . . where, and how, do I start to . . . act like a Christian?

4

HOW DO I ACT LIKE A CHRISTIAN?
or
Wanted: A Christian Character

START WITH A PERSON

The Christian life has always been a mystery to the unsaved. Paul says the unsaved man cannot receive "the things of the Spirit of God, for they are foolishness to him; nor can he know them, because they are spiritually discerned."[1] It need not be a mystery to you, however, for it has now "been revealed to His saints. To them God willed to make known what are the riches of the glory of this mystery among the Gentiles: which is *Christ in you*, the hope of glory."[2]

This whole truth becomes embarrassingly simple, once you see through it. A *Person* saved you, did He not? And it takes a *Person* to keep you day by day.

"I need Thee every hour—stay Thou near by!
Temptations lose their power when Thou art nigh."

Well then, in this matter of producing a Christian character, what makes you think *you* can do it? The blessed Son of God now dwells in you, and it is He who now controls the development of your life.

The secret of Christian character is . . . Jesus Christ! Living within and living out through you, *His* life becomes apparent where once only your failures were seen. This is what Paul means when he exclaims[3]: "Christ lives in me; and the life which I now live in the flesh I live by faith of the Son of God."

SURRENDER TO A PERSON

The Lord Jesus Christ dwells in your heart by His Spirit, but He will control only that portion of your life which you yield to Him. This is the reason behind Paul's words: "I beseech you therefore, brethren, by the mercies of God, that you present your bodies a living sacrifice, holy, acceptable to God, which is your reasonable service."[4]

Present what?

Your body.

Why?

Because His Spirit now dwells in your body, and the only way He can express His life and love is through a yielded instrument. Don't expect the Holy Spirit to transform your heart-house if you refuse to let Him into all the rooms in it! Because you're a Christian, you have a right to all of the Holy Spirit as your birthright;[5] but the big question now is: Does He have all of you?

This need not be a painful experience or something which you must necessarily seek. Right now, if you mean business with God about it, you can bow your head and give over to God the Holy Spirit complete control of yourself—body, soul, and spirit. That is the first step in developing Christian character. Only *He* can develop it, so start by letting *Him* take control.

One big surprise you'll meet about this time is that the things for which you sought so eagerly along the line of Christian character— things like a loving heart, a generous disposition, and a faithful performance of duty—are not an end in themselves, but a result!

The passage that presents this truth is Galatians 5:22, 23. Look it up and read, first of all, the three verses which precede this passage. "Works of the flesh" is the ugly title. We ought constantly to remind ourselves that all the flesh—our old Adam nature—is capable of is dead works; actually, a perversion of the good which we seek—every item on that heartbreaking list is a twisted, perverted opposite of some virtue.

"But," he says, "the fruit of the Spirit is love, joy, peace. . . ."

Fruit, did you say, Paul?

Yes, fruit.

But why change the figure of speech, Paul? You were speaking of the works of the flesh in those three preceding verses. Should you not now speak of the works of the Spirit?

The aged apostle is silent a moment. No, he says, not works, for the Christian life is not mechanical, but vital. The life of the Holy Spirit unites with your life and produces a life product. Christian character is never primarily the things you do—it's the person you are as a result of being indwelt by *the* Person—the Holy Spirit.

COMMUNE WITH A PERSON

The word "communion," when applied to our relationship to God in developing Christian character, has two phases. You'll find them outlined in Philippians 4:6-8.

Paraphrasing Paul's words, we read: Don't worry about anything; pray about everything, and God will give you that miraculous, perfect peace that the world envies but only Christians possess.

The first phase of communion is to *take everything you know about yourself to Him.* "Everything by prayer and supplication." There is absolutely nothing about which you dare not pray. God is GOD—great enough to run the universe and still have time for the most minute detail of your life.

Tell the truth: There are still many things in your life *about which you know*, but which you have never voiced to God in prayer. Either carelessness or fear has kept you from it. Simply, the truth is this: If you want to be different, tell Jesus about it.

The second phase of communion is to *take everything you know about Him . . . to yourself!* You may not realize it, but verse eight is a perfect description of Jesus Christ: "whatsoever things are true,[6] noble,[7] just,[8] pure,[9] lovely,[10] of good report,[11] virtuous,[12] praiseworthy."[13] Now . . . all these things that He is . . . THINK on these things . . . take them to yourself . . . make them part of your life, by faith!

OBEY A PERSON

"Whatever He says to you, do it."[14] Wise-hearted Mary! She knew the secret of success when dealing with our blessed Lord. So did Paul. If you'll turn again to that passage in Philippians 4, you will find him saying in verse 9: "The things which you learned and received and heard and saw in me, these do, and the

God of peace will be with you."

By now you are familiar with the process by which one finds out what God wants him to do. Here it is, carefully delineated for you:

Learned—gained from reading the Word.

Received—gained from experience with God.

Heard—gained from exhortation from the servant of God.

Saw in me—gained from observation of true Christian character in others.

What now? Look carefully at the next word, "do." God will never force you to obey. There comes a time when, after His Spirit has dealt with you and His Word has informed you, that you must *act*, either to obey or to disobey. Obey Him, and you'll experience the blessed fulfillment of the promise given only to those who obey, "The God of peace will be with you." We receive the peace of God when we pray about everything and commit it to Him. But we know the precious awareness of the presence of God only when we obey Him! A number of Scriptures prove this point. Peter, bold in his new experience of the Holy Spirit's power, said: "And we are His witnesses to these things, and so also is the Holy Spirit whom God has given to those who obey Him" (Acts 5:32). Peter *received* the Holy Spirit in answer to the promise of the Father, according to the Word of the Lord

Jesus, but he was *aware* of the Holy Spirit, because he was just then obeying God.

Again, in Matthew 28:19-20, we hear the Lord Jesus saying, "Go therefore . . ."—a definite command. Then, presupposing their obedience, He says, "And lo, I am with you always, even to the end of the age."

Friend, when God is with you—because you are surrendered to Him, communing with Him, obeying Him—*you'll be different*, and people will know it. Read 1 Samuel 3:19, 20.

IMPORTANT COUNSEL

Major on spirituality. Look for the things, the people, the associations in life that will make you more effective as a Christian. Better be ignorant on some of the news of the day, if you must, than miss being the bearer of good news from heaven. Make the rule of your life Philippians 3:10—to know Him, to share His heart, to resemble Him, with the mark of the cross upon you!

Expect people to fail, then they won't disappoint you when they do. By this we mean not cynicism, but an awareness of the fact that Romans 3:23 is absolutely true, all the time. Never hitch your wagon to any earthly star—it will some day flicker and go out. People—the best people—fail sometimes, but Jesus never fails.

"Looking unto Jesus, the author and finisher of our faith!"

Always choose the high road when faced with a choice between two courses of conduct. If there's a better, holier, purer, more generous, more honest way to do anything—take that way!

If there's any doubt about a thing, it's wrong for you. Someone else may do it with a perfectly clear conscience. Let him. If *you* are in doubt, don't touch it. "Whatever is not from faith is sin."[15] That means: Whatever you can't be absolutely sure is the will of God, is wrong. Stay away from it.

Position as a Christian among other Christians depends squarely on your passion for Christ. Strive not to be like brother or sister So-and-so, but to be more like Christ . . . to love Him more devotedly and serve Him more faithfully. You'll rate as a Christian in direct proportion to how much—or how little—Christ dominates your life.

The true Christian is the one who lives his love for Christ all the time. Real love refuses to be pigeonholed! Either it affects all that you are and do, or it is no love at all. Right now, get on your knees and stay there until you can honestly answer the question of John 21:15—"Do you love Me more . . .?" When you love Him supremely, you'll serve Him acceptably. Then

54

Christian character will be not a trial but a triumph—His triumph!

COORDINATE SCRIPTURE FOR
CHAPTER 4

1. But the natural man does not receive the things of the Spirit of God, for they are foolishness to him; nor can he know them, because they are spiritually discerned (1 Corinthians 2:14).

2. The mystery which has been hidden from ages and from generations, but now has been revealed to His saints.
   To them God willed to make known what are the riches of the glory of this mystery among the Gentiles: which is Christ in you, the hope of glory (Colossians 1:26, 27).

3. I have been crucified with Christ; it is no longer I who live, but Christ who lives in me; and the life which I now live in the flesh I live by faith in the Son of God, who loved me and gave Himself for me (Galatians 2:20).

4. I beseech you therefore, brethren, by the mercies of God, that you present your bodies a living sacrifice, holy, acceptable to God, which is your reasonable service (Romans 12:1).

5. But ye are not in the flesh but in the Spirit, if indeed the Spirit of God dwells in you. Now if

anyone does not have the Spirit of Christ, he is not His (Romans 8:9).

Or do you not know that your body is the temple of the Holy Spirit who is in you, whom you have from God, and you are not your own?

For you were bought at a price; therefore glorify God in your body and in your spirit, which are God's (1 Corinthians 6:19, 20).

6. And to the angel of the church in Philadelphia write, "These things says He who is holy, He who is true, 'He who has the key of David, He who opens and no one shuts, and shuts and no one opens' " (Revelation 3:7).

7. But because I tell the truth, you do not believe Me (John 8:45).

8. While he was sitting on the judgment seat, his wife sent to him, saying, "Have nothing to do with that just Man, for I have suffered many things today in a dream because of Him" (Matthew 27:19).

9. And everyone who has this hope in Him purifies himself, just as He is pure (1 John 3:3).

10. His mouth is most sweet, Yes, he is altogether lovely. This is my beloved, And this is my friend, O daughters of Jerusalem! (Song of Solomon 5:16).

11. And they were astonished beyond measure, saying, "He has done all things well. He makes both the deaf to hear and the mute to speak (Mark 7:37).

12. And Jesus, immediately knowing in Himself that power had gone out of Him, turned around in

the crowd and said, "Who touched My clothes? (Mark 5:30).

13. If anyone speaks, let him speak as the oracles of God. If anyone ministers, let him do it as with the ability which God supplies, that in all things God may be glorified through Jesus Christ, to whom belong the glory and dominion forever and ever. Amen (1 Peter 4:11).

14. His mother said to the servants, "Whatever He says to you, do it" (John 2:5).

15. But he who doubts is condemned if he eats, because he does not eat from faith; for whatever is not from faith is sin (Romans 14:23).

Therefore, to him who knows to do good and does not do it to him it is sin (James 4:17).

Christians venerate the Bible—that is no surprise to me. What I can't understand is that so many of them enjoy reading it, talk familiarly of its truths, and really know their way around in its pages. Because I'm now a Christian, I want to have a Christian attitude toward the Word of God, but where do I start reading, how do I study it—in other words, what's the secret that will make the Bible really interesting?

5

WHAT TO DO ABOUT THE BIBLE
or
Holy Book . . . Living Guide: Which?

You already have within you the secret of interest in the Bible. Whether you know it or not, you will always be hungry for the Word of God . . . because you're a Christian! The person who is right with God instinctively loves His Word. "Oh, how I love Your law!" exclaimed the psalmist. "It is my meditation all the day. . . . How sweet are Your words to my taste, Sweeter than honey to my mouth!" (Psalm 119:97, 103).

If "Christ in you, the hope of glory," is the secret of Christian assurance and character, it is also the basic provision for your success with the Word. The *living Word* now dwells in your heart by faith, and His Spirit reminds you moment by moment of your need for the written Word. The Lord Jesus was speaking expressly of your need for the Bible's life-giving truth when He said that the Holy Spirit would "bring to your remembrance all things that I said to you" (John 14:26).

Your business now is to recognize that God has put this holy hunger for the Word in your heart, to know that you will never be satisfied with anything *less* than the Word of God, and to make daily provision for generous portions of the Living Bread.

SOME THINGS YOU SHOULD KNOW

Help yourself to a blessing right here by going over some of the things the Bible does for God's children.

We grow by the Word of God. "As newborn babes," says Peter, "desire the pure milk of the word, that you may grow thereby, if indeed you have tasted that the Lord is gracious" (1 Peter 2:2-3). Are you recently saved? Then you're a babe in Christ, and your first need is to grow. Christians grow through feeding on the Word. More later in this chapter about *how* to do it.

We are changed by the Word. "But we all, with unveiled face, beholding as in a mirror [the Bible is God's heavenly looking glass where we see reflected our needs and His glory] the glory of the Lord, are being transformed into the same image from glory to glory, just as by the Spirit of the Lord" (2 Corinthians 3:18). Would you be more like Jesus? Read the Bible!

We are cleansed by the Word. "How can a

young man cleanse his way? By taking heed according to Your word (Psalm 119:9)[1]

We are kept by the Word. "Your word I have hidden in my heart, That I might not sin against You" (Psalm 119:11).

We share God's life through the Word. "The words that I speak to you are spirit, and they are life."[2]

We defeat the devil through the Word. "And they overcame him by the blood of the Lamb *and by the word* of their testimony, and they did not love their lives to the death" (Revelation 12:11). "The sword of the Spirit, which is the word of God" (Ephesians 6:17).

We win souls through preaching the Word. Christ "preached the word to them."[3] The early church preached the Word.[4] God promises to bless His Word—not your opinions.

We base our faith on the Word, *and produce faith* in others by proclaiming the Word.[5]

Our eternal authority is the Word,[6] therefore we speak confidently and authoritatively as did the prophets when they said, "Thus saith the Lord."

Every needed blessing is in the Word.[7] Here are just a few from Psalm 119: Cleansing, quickening, strengthening, establishing, comfort, hope, guidance, order, pleasant meditation, joy, understanding, deliverance. You need never lack for anything while you have the Word of God!

Cultivate a regard for the Bible as being literally The . . . Word . . . of . . . God. No longer merely a holy book, it must now become the very stuff of which your moral and spiritual fabric is woven. When you were unsaved, you could quibble about whether or not the Word was important. Now . . . that point is forever settled. It *is* God's Word—treat it as such.

Get a good Bible, with readable print. Nothing discourages the beginner more than having to struggle with sticking pages and fine type. Your eyes blur, your mind grows weary; and before you realize it, the devil has won another victory. Get a good Bible! The money you invest in it will be repaid times without number.

Make up your mind that you are going to read your Bible every day from now until you get to Glory. You expect to eat pretty regularly until you leave this world, don't you? Let's have as much sense about our spiritual condition as we try to show in maintaining our physical bodies! Believe me, friend, many a life has been wrecked by neglect of this truth: You cannot live successfully and forget the Bible. You *must* feed your soul![8]

Learn to *eat* the Word of God. Jeremiah says: "Your words were found, and I ate them, And Your word was to me the joy and rejoicing of my heart; For I am called by Your name, O Lord God of hosts" (Jeremiah 15:16). How do you eat the Word? Well, what happens when you take physical food into your body? That little boy drinks a glass of milk. His body takes white milk and turns it into white teeth, and blue eyes, and yellow hair, and strong bones, and a clear, ruddy complexion. What he eats becomes part of his life.

Here's how to eat the Word: Take your Bible and open it to the book through which you happen to be reading. Get on your knees, and ask God in Jesus' name to speak to you from His Word. Read and reread the passage until, in the stillness of your heart, God the Holy Spirit says something . . . from the Word . . . just for you! When He does, get paper and a pen and write it down. Now, still on your knees before God, pray back to Him what He said to your heart. Pray, on the basis of God's Word to you, until your very soul is aflame with the message. Then arise and proceed to put into action that which God has put into your life. Share with someone as soon as possible the blessings you received through eating the Word.

Make a time each day when you will read the Word of God, the earlier in your day the better. The longer you put off getting into the Word, the less value in eternity will your day have. And be very sure, if you do not make a place for the Word, you will never have a consistent Christian life. Invariably the up-and-then-down-ers, the feeble brethren and sisters who never make the grade for God, are the folk who either willfully, or stupidly, refuse to make a place and time in their daily schedule for God's Word.

Everything in the Bible has some connection with the Lord Jesus and His work for, in, and through the believer. Always read your Bible with this in mind: How will I find Christ revealed in the Word today?

Read the Bible sensibly, as you would a textbook.

Read it earnestly, as a lawyer scans a contract: each word was put into the Bible by the Holy Spirit and has its own definite meaning for you.

Read God's Word ardently, as a lover reads a love letter. The Bible is God's love letter to you: "Yes, I have loved you with an everlasting love," He says. "Therefore with lovingkindness I have drawn you" (Jeremiah 31:3).

When you have read it, speak enthusiastically of the Bible to your friends and acquaintances. Nothing is more conducive to joy and real growth in grace than speaking out that which you learned in the secret place.

Start reading and studying the easier portions of the Bible first. The gospel of John, for instance, was expressly written to lead folk to Christ (John 20:31) and presents Him in a most wonderful manner. The book of Acts tells how the early church was formed and how any normal church operates, tells of missionary endeavors, and creates a soul-winner's vision in the hearts of those who read it. The book of Romans breaks down in detail the truth of the gospel—*why* you need a Savior, *how* you are saved, and *what* happens after you are saved. This will give you a start. After that, you're on your own!

Build your life around the Bible. NOTHING WILL EVER BE SO IMPORTANT TO YOU AS THE WORD OF GOD! No other book, magazine, newspaper, activity, recreation, friend, or loved one will ever have the right to demand so much or the power to contribute so much in your life as the Scriptures.

Neglect the Bible, and you neglect your own soul. Read and obey it, and you enhance your own life while blessing countless others.

HOW TO "BREAK OPEN" THE
WORD OF GOD

Always—ALWAYS—begin your Bible study with earnest prayer for God's enlightenment and guidance: "Open my eyes, that I may see wondrous things from Your law" (Psalm

119:18). The Holy Spirit takes time to say that "the natural man does not receive the things of the Spirit of God," and "they that are in the flesh cannot please God," and "without faith it is impossible to please Him." So if you would have God's approval on your Bible study, better come to Him first in prayer about it.

Remember that the main subject of the Bible is redemption . . . and that the main Person of redemption is the Lord Jesus Christ. Sensible Bible study, then, will *look for references to Him* in every page of Holy Writ. In the Old Testament, you will find Him pictured in ritual (Tabernacle and Levitical sacrifices), in types (people who foreshadowed Christ by their lives), and in prophetic truth (utterances which point directly to either the first or second coming of Christ).

In the New Testament, you will see the various aspects of His ministry beautifully depicted by the varying approaches of the gospels. W. H. Griffith Thomas says: "We may consider four passages beginning with 'Behold' and note:

a) Behold a King. Isa. 32:1 (Matthew)

b) Behold My Servant. Isa. 42:1 (Mark)

c) Behold the Man. John 19:5 (Luke)

d) Behold your God. Isa. 40:9 (John)[9]

"The aim is one and the same, but their methods and aspects differ. St. Matthew demonstrates; St. Mark depicts; St. Luke declares; St. John describes. St. Matthew demonstrates (based on Old Testament) the coming of an expected Saviour; St. Mark depicts the life of a powerful Saviour; St. Luke declares the grace of a human Saviour; St. John describes the possession of a personal Saviour."*

Everything in the Bible has its own beautiful relationship to our Lord Jesus Christ: "Beginning at Moses and all the Prophets, He expounded to them in all the Scriptures the things concerning Himself" (Luke 24:27).

Here are some other things you will find helpful in your reading and study of God's Word:

1. Read entire books of the Bible, and find their main theme and message.

2. Follow individual life stories in the Bible, and you will discover some most fascinating biography.

3. Follow through the development of a truth or a doctrine. Mark with a certain color, for instance, every verse that deals with God's grace or His love.

4. Look for casual references to people—references that give an index to their character. Of Absalom, for example, all the Holy Spirit could say was that he was handsome, had beautiful

*Methods of Bible Study, by W. H. Griffith Thomas.

hair, and cut it once a year! (2 Samuel 14:25-26). What an indication of supreme vanity.

5. Look for verbs denoting action. After your first casual reading of a passage, go back and underscore all the words that denote action of any kind. You will be amazed by the clarity of the message thus relayed.

6. Read and reread a chapter until you are able to pick out its theme, topic sentence, best verse, and lasting lesson. Anywhere from six to twenty readings are indicated here, but when you're through, you'll have the chapter, and it will have you!

7. Remember: ALWAYS FIND OUT WHAT THE BIBLE SAYS BEFORE YOU TRY TO TELL WHAT IT MEANS. Generally, when you know what the Word says about any given question, you will have no uncertainty over your own course of conduct.

SUPREMELY IMPORTANT

You must—YOU MUST—resolve to obey the Word as you read it. Just as neglect of the Word can cut the throat of your Christian endeavor, so a disobedient heart and mind will tune out heaven's message and leave only the static of your own mental meanderings. "You are my friends," Jesus said, "if you do whatever I command you" (John 15:14). "We are His witnesses," said Peter, "and so also is the Holy Spirit whom God has given *to those who obey Him*" (Acts 5:32). Let your daily prayer be, "Lord, while I read Thy Word, give me wisdom to understand (James 1:5) and grace and courage to obey!"

COORDINATE SCRIPTURE FOR CHAPTER 5

1. You are already clean because of the word which I have spoken to you (John 15:3).

That He might sanctify and cleanse it with the washing of the water by the word (Ephesians 5:26).

2. It is the Spirit who gives life; the flesh profits nothing. The words that I speak to you are spirit, and they are life (John 6:63).

3. Immediately many gathered together, so that there was no longer room to receive them, not even near the door. And He preached the word to them (Mark 2:2).

4. So when they had testified and preached the word of the Lord, they returned to Jerusalem, preaching the gospel in many villages of the Samaritans (Acts 8:25).

And when they arrived at Salamis, they preached the word of God in the synagogues of the Jews. They also had John as their assistant (Acts 13:5).

Now when they had preached the word in Perga, they went down to Attalia (Acts 14:25).

5. So then faith comes by hearing, and hearing by the word of God (Romans 10:17).

6. Forever, O Lord, Your word is settled in heaven (Psalm 119:89).

7. As His divine power has given to us all things that pertain to life and godliness, through the knowledge of Him who called us by glory and virtue, by which have been given to us exceedingly great and precious promises, that through these you may be partakers of the divine nature, having escaped the corruption that is in the world through lust (2 Peter 1:3-4).

8. As newborn babes, desire the pure milk of the word, that you may grow thereby (1 Peter 2:2).

9. Behold, a king will reign in righteousness, And princes will rule with justice (Isaiah 32:1).

Behold! My Servant whom I uphold, My Elect One in whom My soul delights! I have put My Spirit upon Him; He will bring forth justice to the Gentiles (Isaiah 42:1).

Then Jesus came out, wearing the crown of thorns and the purple robe. And Pilate said to them, "Behold the Man!" (John 19:5).

O Zion, you who bring good tidings, get up into the high mountain; O Jerusalem, you who bring good tidings, lift up your voice with strength, lift it up, be not afraid; say to the cities of Judah, "Behold your God!" (Isaiah 40:9).

Prayer mystifies me. Some seem to agonize in prayer . . . others are quiet in their devotions. Some have a set form of approach to God, others are most informal in their address to the Deity. Some speak of "praying through," while others calmly say that they commit everything to the Lord.

Loud or soft . . . short or long . . . agony or litany—where do I fit in?

6

HOW CAN I PRAY?

Emphatically, prayer is *not* a polite speech to the Deity. One is convinced that when the books are opened, many a humanly acceptable prayer will be found among the "wood, hay, straw"[1] because it was merely the effort of the flesh to cultivate favor with God.

WHAT PRAYER IS

Prayer is a cry. The physician expects the newborn babe to cry out as first evidence of life. If it does not cry, he shakes or spanks it to produce a cry. If it continues silent, it will soon be dead.

Here is a singular thing. Peter says that we are "newborn babes,"[2] and yet we never expect new converts to do the very thing that a babe ought to do: cry. "Because you are sons," says Paul, "God has sent forth the Spirit of His Son into your hearts, crying out, 'Abba, Father!' "

(Galatians 4:6). *Abba* is the orientalism for our word "papa." It is the cry of a childlike heart that does not know much, but knows it is alive and that it needs the tender care of its heavenly Father.

Again, Paul says, "For you did not receive the spirit of bondage again to fear, but you received the Spirit of adoption by whom we cry out, 'Abba, Father!' " (Romans 8:15).

God respects the cry of the converted heart. There are literally hundreds of references proving this fact. Here are a couple: "He will deliver the needy when he cries, The poor also, and him who has no helper" (Psalm 72:12). "This poor man cried out, and the Lord heard him, And saved him out of all his troubles" (Psalm 34:6).

I cannot speak strongly enough about this matter. Your birthright as a Christian is that warm, tender heart toward God . . . that cry down deep in your spirit that reaches its poor mute hands out to God and pleads more eloquently than the best of human words. Cherish that cry. Let it come out. Let it make itself heard in every one of your prayers, either private or public. Let us have done with cold, formal, heartless, pagan praying. It grieves the heart of God and leaves our own lives more poverty-stricken than they were before.

Do you know what that cry is? It is the

74

blessed Holy Spirit in your heart, calling out to God. Because you *are* a Christian, He indwells you.[3] And because you frequently do not know what to say, He says it for you in the language that God Almighty understands. Look at these beautiful words: "Likewise the Spirit also helps in our weaknesses. For we do not know what we should pray for as we ought, but the Spirit Himself makes intercession for us with groanings which cannot be uttered. Now He who searches the hearts knows what the mind of the Spirit is, because He makes intercession for the saints according to the will of God" (Romans 8:26-27).

Let us look honestly at this matter. You are newly converted—a babe in Christ. Sure, you don't know what to say, or how to say it. But deep within you there dwells One who does know and whose business it is to express the very yearnings of the heart of God through your heart. That's the cry... the cry of the Holy Spirit. Prayer is a cry—His cry—to God through you!

Humanly speaking, prayer is often simply a call for help. "Call to Me, and I will answer you, and show you great and mighty things, which you do not know" (Jeremiah 33:3), is our encouragement.

A call means earnest desire, specific desire, determined and oftentimes desperate desire—

and, thank God, a call to Him means an answer. "And it shall come to pass that whoever calls on the name of the Lord shall be saved. . . . For 'whoever calls upon the name of the Lord shall be saved' " (Joel 2:32, Romans 10:13).

Form the habit of calling upon God at every occasion of need in your life. A bowed head, an open heart, and the simple words, "Lord Jesus, help me now!" can mean the difference between defeat and victory.

Prayer involves confession and cleansing. "If I regard iniquity in my heart, the Lord will not hear," said the psalmist soberly (Psalm 66:18). Isaiah sounds the same warning: "Behold, the Lord's hand is not shortened, that it cannot save; nor His ear heavy, that it cannot hear. But your iniquities have separated you from your God; and your sins have hidden His face from you, so that He will not hear" (Isaiah 59:1, 2).

Make up your mind to this now: I can never hide known sin in my heart and expect to get my prayers answered.

Do you know how to get rid of sin? Confess it and forsake it. "He who covers his sins will not prosper, but whoever confesses and forsakes them will have mercy" (Proverbs 28:13). "If we confess our sins, He is faithful and just to forgive us our sins and to cleanse us from all unrighteousness" (1 John 1:9). Just tell God the truth about your sin: "Lord, I lied, or I cheated, or I stole, or I lost my temper." Specific confession will bring specific cleansing. (And, of course, when you have sinned against an individual, you'll go get right with that person, too.)

Like everything else in the Christian life, prayer must be Christ-centered. The disciples, beginners in the school of prayer, were told: "Until now you have asked nothing in My name. Ask, and you will receive, that your joy may be full" (John 16:24). Why is this? Look at the preceding verse: "Most assuredly, I say to you, whatever you ask the Father in My name He will give you."

"In Jesus' name," we say when we pray—why?

Because that is the saving Name: "And you shall call His name Jesus, for He will save His people from their sins" (Matthew 1:21).

Because He is the only one through whom you can come to God: "No one comes to the Father except through Me," He said.[4]

Because He is the one whose work it is today tenderly to represent you in the Father's presence: "Therefore He is also able to save to the uttermost those who come to God through Him, since He ever lives to make intercession for them" (Hebrews 7:25).

If Christ is the "everything" of salvation and life—and He is!—then He must also be the very heart of all your praying. Pray with a deep dependence on your living Lord and Intercessor, and you will always touch the heart of God.

THINGS TO REMEMBER

1. Have a time and place for daily prayer. Someone has well said, "If you do not have a time for prayer, you will soon not have time for prayer!" There is some place in your home, even though it be just a coal shed or a clothes closet, where you can get alone with God. Don't worry about discomfort—you pray better when you are not so comfortable as to be half asleep. Remember, Jonah prayed effectively even in the belly of the fish. Location is relatively unimportant, but a definite time and place are all-important.

2. Have a prayer list—an agenda of things you want from God. Help yourself to a blessing and increasing richness of life by writing down the things you need from heaven's storehouse. Then go after them, one by one, earnestly, in faith, and in complete dependence upon your Lord. Save that list, and check off the answers when they come. You'll receive a real thrill when you are able to write "Hallelujah" and the date beside some glorious answer to prayer on your prayer list. Always remember

James 5:16-18. Elijah—an ordinary man, beset by ordinary temptations, but with a real faith in an Almighty God, prayed earnestly . . . and got an answer. He prayed again . . . and God answered again. No coincidence here—just a commonplace person praying to a mighty God.

3. Pray on the basis of God's Word. "Now this is the confidence that we have in Him, that if we ask anything according to His will, He hears us. And if we know that He hears us, whatever we ask, we know that we have the petitions that we have asked of Him" (1 John 5:14-15).

Anything according to His will—where do you find the will of God? In His Word, of course. Search the Word of God until you find your own peculiar "praying ground"—a promise or a portion that is particularly applicable to your case—then pray on the authority and basis of that Scripture. Friend, the answers will come trooping down from the throne of grace!

4. Maintain a quiet time daily with God. This involves bowing quietly and asking for consecration on the Word . . . reading until God speaks definitely to YOU . . . writing down what He said (if you can't write it succinctly, you haven't got it!) . . . then praying it back to Him: "This, Lord, is what Thou didst say to me." One more thing: Share what God said to you with someone else as quickly as you can.

Praying it and telling it will fasten the truth in your heart and character.

5. Avoid forms and habitual expressions in prayer. Remember you are talking to a wonderful PERSON. Think how embarrassed you would be if you followed the "dear heavenly Father" repetition idea in speaking to a neighbor: "Good morning, dear Mr. Jones. How are you, dear Mr. Jones? Nice day, dear Mr. Jones, etc., etc." There is no substitute for sense, courtesy, and thought in prayer.

6. Make prayer the springboard for obedience. Nothing will stultify your prayer life so much as the unwillingness to do what God whispers to your heart while you wait before Him. "But be doers of the word, and not hearers only, deceiving yourselves" (James 1:22).

7. Look for an answer after you have prayed. A classic example of this truth is found in 1 Kings 18:41-46: Elijah . . . the victory on Mount Carmel . . . the promise of rain . . . the ground still parched and dry while the sun blazed down overhead. Elijah goes to prayer. While he prays, he sends his servant to look toward the sea. "So he went up and looked, and said, 'There is nothing.' And seven times he said, 'Go again.' Then it came to pass the seventh time, that he said, 'There is a cloud, as small as a man's hand, rising out of the sea.'

Now it happened in the meantime that the sky became black with clouds and wind, and there was a heavy rain."

Faith is just expecting God to act like God! Elijah had prayed, and now he expected a Godlike answer. Simple . . . keep praying and expecting until the answer arrives!

8. Never quit. God likes to have His people "make mention of the Lord, do not keep silent, and give Him no rest."[5] The Lord Jesus said, "men always ought to pray and not lose heart."[6] Paul said, "Praying always,"[7] and, "Pray without ceasing" (1 Thessalonians 5:17).

Never stop praying when you feel like stopping—Satan is just tempting you and trying to cheat you of a blessing. The time when you feel the weakest, and the most helpless, and when you realize that you are praying so poorly— THAT IS THE TIME TO KEEP ON. YOU ARE JUST ON THE THRESHOLD OF BLESSING! Pray through. Pray until the Holy Spirit has told you in your heart of hearts that God has heard and will answer. Then rise, praise Him, and expect the answer. It will come.

9. Expect the Holy Spirit to pray through *your* personality—not someone else. Never try to pray like another person. If you do, you will turn out to be nothing but a pious fraud. Avoid "ministerial tones" and the "pious whine" like the plague. Strive to be perfectly natural, utter-

ly sincere, and completely yielded to the blessed Spirit of God. Then, no matter what form your prayer assumes, it will really be YOU praying in the power of the Spirit.

COORDINATE SCRIPTURE FOR CHAPTER 6

1. Now if anyone builds on this foundation with gold, silver, precious stones, wood, hay, straw, each one's work will become manifest (1 Corinthians 3:12-13).

2. As newborn babes, desire the pure milk of the word, that you may grow thereby (1 Peter 2:2).

3. Or do you not know that your body is the temple of the Holy Spirit who is in you, whom you have from God, and you are not your own?

For you were bought at a price; therefore glorify God in your body and in your spirit, which are God's (1 Corinthians 6:19-20).

4. Jesus said to him, "I am the way, the truth, and the life. No one comes to the Father except through Me" (John 14:6).

5. I have set watchmen on your walls, O Jerusalem, who shall never hold their peace day or night. You who make mention of the Lord, do not keep silent, and give Him no rest till He establishes and till He makes Jerusalem a praise in the earth (Isaiah 62:6-7).

6. Then He spoke a parable to them, that men always ought to pray and not lose heart (Luke 18:1).

7. Praying always with all prayer and supplication in the Spirit, being watchful to this end with all perseverance and supplication for all saints (Ephesians 6:18).

Other Christians are always talking about "witnessing." I wince when I think about barging into somebody's life, preaching to him, and probably embarrassing us both. Furthermore, I don't like the ostentatious, show-off kind of Christian who hides his not-so-subtle bragging under a thin cloak of testimony. Maybe I could just keep quiet about it . . . I wonder . . . do I have to speak out for Christ?

7

DO I HAVE TO TESTIFY?

First reaction to this question is: "How can you help it?" True testimony or witnessing consists of vastly more than the spoken word. If you're real, you'll be bound to say something for Christ.

Please bear carefully in mind: Whether you are in the will of God or not, whether saved or unsaved, you are most emphatically giving a witness all the time—a witness to *whatever rules your life.* Like it or not, some of us are witnessing to our selfishness, our laziness, our lusts, our sub rosa love of the world, our shallowness, vanity, and pride—oh, a thousand other things!

You never successfully conceal anything. You are witness to whatever you *are* down deep in your heart. "For out of the abundance of the heart the mouth speaks."[1]

The increasing tendency to leave all effective

witnessing to the clergy, or to the eager-beaver type of Christian layfolk, is based not upon a valid distinction between talents, but upon sheer laziness or lack of true Christian experience.

Notice the significance of Acts 1:8 in this connection. The disciples had so far been witnesses only to their own cowardice and fear; to their low viewpoint of the Kingdom as a restore-Israel type of program; and to their utterly insular point of view, so far as help for the world was concerned. Now the Lord Jesus tells them, "There is going to be a new power that rules your lives. You will be controlled by the Holy Spirit. He will constrain you to speak of Me . . . not only where you are now, but reaching out into Judea and Samaria, then unto the uttermost part of the world."

Successful witnessing never was a matter of determination on the part of the early church. They never did urge each other to testify. It was not a matter of conscience even. They simply reacted normally to the lordship of the Holy Spirit. They were genuine. Even in their failure before and immediately after Calvary, they were utterly unposed. Similarly, when the blessed Spirit of God came upon them and began to speak through them, it was not a matter of trying but of glad surrender to His presence and power.

We border on the rankest hypocrisy when we *try* to do anything that takes a miracle to be genuine.

Use your will where it belongs—in willing to do God's will, in determining by God's grace to pray every day and read the Word of God regularly, and in willing to turn away from every appearance of evil.

Rely on *His will* and *His Spirit* when it comes to the matter of a relationship so important that it involves the salvation of a precious soul. Why, do you think, did the Lord Jesus emphasize so often the fact that the Holy Spirit would be given to guide, to bring to remembrance His words, to put proper words into disciples' trembling lips, to teach them what to say? Was it not that the Lord Jesus knows the awful impotence of the human brain, the perversity of the human tongue, and the utter impossibility of changing lives by mere talk?

A posed witness is a falsehood. The best witness is spontaneous. What you are will lead to what you say. If what you are is low-grade, sinful, worldly, carnal, self-centered, then *you are now witnessing to that fact* and soiling with guilty fingers all the lives you touch!

Get in touch with the Lord Jesus Christ.

By prayer—real prayer that breaks your heart and moistens your eyes.

By eating the Word (Jeremiah 15:16), a process that takes some time every day.

By consciously cultivating the love of your Savior and casting out everything that you know grieves Him.

By consciously surrendering to the Holy Spirit (Ephesians 5:18; Romans 12:1).

God does not want your talents—not even the gift of gab!

He wants you, in a brokenhearted, sincere, now-and-forever kind of surrender that will make an effective Christian witness out of *everything* you say or do.

Having said all this, here are some pointers for successful witnessing:

1. Get over the mental hurdle involved in "talking religion" to people. Actually you talk to folk about every conceivable subject from morning to night. The only trouble about speaking for Christ is that you are unfamiliar with the subject, and so do not speak without restraint, but rather with some degree of embarrassment. Resolve to be willing to speak naturally of the greatest subject in the world, the Lord Jesus Christ, whenever you have opportunity to choose your own subject of conversation. (On this matter, see *Taking Men Alive*, by Trumbull.)

2. Fill your mind and heart with the Word of God. "I will speak of Your testimonies . . . and

will not be ashamed."[2] You speak naturally and unposedly only about material that has gotten down into your subconscious, or below-routine level of thinking. Hide God's Word in your heart, and you will find yourself speaking of it, living by it, illustrating its truth by your character and conduct, and, in general, having a highly effective witness as a result.

Question: How long has it been since you mastered a Scripture verse? Try one today, and say it over at intervals all day long; then review it once a day for seven weeks. At the end of that time you will have the Scripture, but—more important—it will also have you! (Write to the Navigators, Colorado Springs, Colorado, for material on hiding God's Word in your heart.)

3. Begin each day with prayer for God's guidance, and form the habit of watching throughout the day for the people God will send to you for your ministry to them. He knows whom you can help, and He can put you in touch with them.

4. Always rely on the Holy Spirit to tell you what to say. Pray before you begin conversations or even a telephone chat with some unknown caller. The Holy Spirit will lead you to use a Scripture, a telling thought that, quite unknown to you, will be the final link in the

chain of events that leads to someone's salvation.

Never depend upon smart logic or smooth conversation to do the work either of conviction or conversion. Only the Holy Spirit using the Word can do that. Let Him.[3]

5. Always press gently for some action NOW. It may be only a word of prayer where you are talking together . . . or it may be you will have the joy of leading your friend directly to Jesus.

A demonstration (Romans 12:2*b*) without a sale (Acts 2:37) is worth very little. We are to prove what is good and acceptable and perfect, namely, the will of God in Christ (John 6:40). A "sale" for the Christian soul-winner is that point at which your prospect is genuinely convicted by the Holy Spirit, senses his need, and asks for help. Get *some* action toward that desired result always before you leave.

6. Follow through. One contact may mean attention; another appreciation; but a third often means decision.

7. Soul-winning is a miracle. To try it in the energy of the flesh is fraudulent and sinful. God must do it through you, and He will, on the basis of Colossians 2:6 and Philippians 2:13. You received Christ by faith, now let Him operate through you by faith. When Jesus wins a soul, the work is well done! (See John 17:6-12.)

COORDINATE SCRIPTURE FOR
CHAPTER 7

1. Brood of vipers! How can you, being evil, speak good things? For out of the abundance of the heart the mouth speaks (Matthew 12:34).

2. I will speak of Your testimonies also before kings, and will not be ashamed (Psalm 119:46).

3. So then faith comes by hearing, and hearing by the word of God (Romans 10:17).

Nevertheless I tell you the truth. It is to your advantage that I go away; for if I do not go away, the Helper will not come to you; but if I depart, I will send Him to you.

And when He has come, He will convict the world of sin, and of righteousness, and of judgment (John 16:7-8).

If I am fully surrendered will I have to become a preacher or a missionary? How will I know to what field God is calling me? How can I know I am in the will of God?

8

WHAT SHALL I DO WITH MY LIFE?

First of all, surrender it absolutely to God without qualification or reservation (Rom. 12:1).[1]

The best way to wreck your life and break your heart is by an incomplete surrender (compare Acts 5:1-11).[2]

The secret of unanswered prayer is incomplete surrender (James 4:3).[3]

The question we must ask is not, "*How* will God use me?" but "Am I usable?"

Don't expect particular guidance without general surrender.

Do you know *how* to *surrender* to God? The secret is found in Luke 14:33: "Whoever of you does not forsake all that he has cannot be My disciple." That word *forsake* means to give up all claim to a thing or person. The way to surrender to God is to hand all that you have and are over to Him—forsake it.

Get a number of slips of paper. Write on one

the amount of money you possess. On another your car. On another your family. On another your house. Continue until you have made a complete list of your dear ones and possessions. Last of all, write on one slip of paper the word, "Myself."

Now you are ready. Take those slips of paper one at a time and—if you really mean business with God—hand them over to Him. "Here, Lord, is my home, my car, my money, my dear ones, myself!"

Oh, to surrender to God! The surrendered life is the life God can use.

Start to live the kind of life God can bless, where you are. Don't wait until next month or next year for the opportunity that may make you great. God will only use the clean, yielded vessel (2 Timothy 2:21).[4] Start being that kind of a vessel now.

Read up on, and pray about, the needs of the world. You will be amazed at how little you know about the great missionary harvest fields of the world. Take a day to read about Africa and to pray for it. Another for India, and another for China. Still another for South America, and so on. By informing your mind, and intelligently obeying Luke 10:2, you give the Holy Spirit something to work on. Remember: Jesus never asked you to pray for a call. He *did* say: "Pray the Lord of the harvest to send out laborers into His harvest." Start there, and let the rest be up to God.

Make a list of your talents and possibilities, and pray over them, asking God to reveal to you what field of endeavor you are best fitted for. Nothing is worse than a misfit, stumbling along trying to make a go of Christian service for which he is obviously not prepared. Similarly, there is nothing more bitter than the cry of a person who realizes too late that he should have been in the ministry or on the mission field but got sidetracked into business or homemaking instead.

Get to work for God NOW. Start in your home, dealing with unsaved loved ones; consider your school or office or shop a place where you can serve and glorify God. In your church, be faithful in attendance and in keeping commitments (God will never use a slacker); be loyal to your pastor and enthusiastic in inviting others to church. You may not be able to preach . . . but you can give out tracts and invitations to the services. When souls are won in this way, you will surely share in the reward at the judgment seat of Christ.

Consider the possibility of Bible school or a Bible-centered college, no matter what field you plan to enter. Mechanic or maestro, banker or bookworm, preacher or painter, you'll do better in your work after having spent two or more years with THE BOOK. "The fear of the Lord is the beginning of wisdom."

Do *right*. There is always a right thing to do. You may have many excuses and rationalizations for getting your own way, but when you meet the piercing eyes of the Lord Jesus, you will wish you had done the right thing. DO RIGHT. God will bless you and use you in it. "You meet him who rejoices and does righteousness, who remembers You in Your ways" (Isaiah 64:5).

Above all, depend on God for every step. "Trust in the Lord with all your heart, and lean not on your own understanding. In all your ways acknowledge Him, and He shall direct your paths" (Proverbs 3:5-6). God can make every hour, every day, a success. And what is a successful life but a series of successful days? Let the Holy Spirit guide. There are no regrets when He is in control.

ADMONITIONS

Always remember that your one business as a Christian is to aid in completing the evangelization of the world. "Into all the world . . . the gospel to every creature" is still the command of the Captain of our salvation. Your mind and heart will never go stale, your usefulness will constantly enlarge, if you keep a missionary vision bright and clear.

Never tolerate sin in your life. No day should go by without your being "prayed and confessed up to date." You may never see the morning light! A little sin leads to more sin, and before you know it, your joy is clouded, your testimony is ruined, and the Holy Spirit is grieved. Keep under the blood of Jesus . . . walk in the light, and fulfill 1 John 1:7.

It is dangerous to trifle with God. Remember Ananias and Sapphira (Acts 5). Remember Gehazi (2 Kings 5:20-27). Remember King Saul 1 Samuel 15:23). Remember Lot's wife (Genesis 19:26). You may pay *with your life* for refusing to judge your sins (1 Corinthians 11:28-32)!

Always follow through in obeying what God told you when your knees were bent and your eyes were wet with tears. Never yield to cold-hearted rationalization that attempts to get your own way at the expense of God's will. You *may convince yourself*, but you'll still be wrong if you forsake the counsel He gave you in the sanctuary of your soul. Keep a tender conscience, and dare to obey what God tells you in the time of prayer. Remember: There are no regrets when He leads!

1. I beseech you therefore, brethren, by the mercies of God, that you present your bodies a living sacrifice, holy, acceptable to God, which is your reasonable service (Romans 12:1).

2. But a certain man named Ananias, with Sapphira his wife, sold a possession.

And he kept back part of the proceeds, his wife also being aware of it, and brought a certain part and laid it at the apostles' feet.

But Peter said, "Ananias, why has Satan filled your heart to lie to the Holy Spirit, and keep back part of the price of the land for yourself?

"While it remained, was it not your own? And after it was sold, was it not in your own control? Why have you conceived this thing in your heart? You have not lied to men but to God."

And Ananias, hearing these words, fell down and breathed his last. So great fear came upon all those who heard these things.

And the young men arose and wrapped him up, carried him out, and buried him.

Now it was about three hours later when his wife came in, not knowing what had happened.

And Peter answered her, "Tell me whether you sold the land for so much?" And she said, "Yes, for so much."

Then Peter said to her, "How is it that you have agreed together to test the Spirit of the Lord? Look, the feet of those who have buried your husband are at the door, and they will carry you out."

Then immediately she fell down at his feet and breathed her last. And the young men came in and found her dead, and carrying her out, buried her by her husband.

So great fear came upon all the church and upon all who heard these things (Acts 5:1-11).

3. You ask and do not receive, because you ask amiss, that you may spend it on your pleasures (James 4:3).

4. Therefore if anyone cleanses himself from the latter, he will be a vessel for honor, sanctified and useful for the Master, prepared for every good work (2 Timothy 2:21).

Now that I believe, where shall I draw the line in daily conduct? How can I know what is right and wrong? Can I take without question the ethics of my elders and other Christian friends? On the other hand, dare I disregard old-line standards? After all, who is to say whether I am holy or worldly—what makes the difference?

9

WORLDLINESS—AND WHAT TO DO ABOUT IT

You may as well face the facts: If you're born again, you are a different person. "Therefore, if anyone is in Christ, he is a new creation."[1]

You have a new nature—the heavenly nature, begotten of God in you by the Holy Spirit. "But you are not in the flesh but in the Spirit, if indeed the Spirit of God dwells in you. Now if anyone does not have the Spirit of Christ, he is not His" (Romans 8:9).

You have a new citizenship—in a heavenly country: "For our citizenship is in heaven, from which we also eagerly wait for the Savior, the Lord Jesus Christ" (Philippians 3:20).

You are moving toward a new destiny: "Who will transform our lowly body that it may be conformed to His glorious body, according to the working by which He is able even to subdue all things to Himself" (Philippians 3:21).

You are a pilgrim, not a resident: "Beloved, I beg you as sojourners and pilgrims, abstain from fleshly lusts which war against the soul" (1 Peter 2:11).

You have enlisted under a new Captain[2] and are engaged in a new kind of warfare.[3]

You have a new obligation—not to live after the flesh (old nature), but for God's glory.[4]

You have a new status—dead indeed to sin but alive to God.[5]

You belong to a new family and have new relatives: "But as many as received Him, to them He gave the right to become children of God, even to those who believe on His name. . . . Now, therefore, you are no longer strangers and foreigners, but fellow citizens with the saints and members of the household of God" (John 1:12; Ephesians 2:19).

You have a new occupation—to glorify God. "For you were bought at a price; therefore glorify God in your body and in your spirit, which are God's (1 Corinthians 6:20). Therefore, whether you eat or drink, or whatever you do, do all to the glory of God (1 Corinthians 10:31). And whatever you do, do it heartily, as to the Lord and not to men (Colossians 3:23). Created in Christ Jesus for good works, which God prepared beforehand that we should walk in them.[6] I want you to affirm constantly, that those who have believed in God should be careful to maintain good works."[7]

You will never be the same again—*never.* Try

to explain it, rationalize it as you will, a Christian is different from unsaved people because he has been born again. God says so, and it is so.

If your Christianity is just a profession that can fit elastically over all forms of compromise, friend—you're lost! Get down on your knees, and ask God to save you for Jesus' sake!

Another thing you may as well face is this: The world knows you are different since you've been born again.

Paul said, you remember, "Lord, they know that in every synagogue I imprisoned and beat those who believe on You. And when the blood of Your martyr Stephen was shed, I also was standing by consenting to his death."[8]

Yes, they know. They know what you were, and what you are. They watch your every move to see whether you are real or a sham. They listen to see whether your speech betrays the accent of Heaven or the old words and phrases. They know—and they expect you to measure up.

When you compromise and play with the world, the most surprised person of all is the worldling. He may not have understood you ("In regard to these, they think it strange that you do not run with them in the same flood of dissipation, speaking evil of you" [1 Peter 4:4]), and he may have hated you ("Because you are not of the world, but I chose you out of the world, therefore the world hates you"[9]), but he will be surprised and disappointed when you lower Christ's blood-stained banner into the dust and stoop to become a spiritual quisling when you could have been a conqueror!

Think through, now, in your own heart and mind, these facts:

*If I'm born again, I'm different, and will never be the same.

*The world knows I'm different, expects me to be different, and will be surprised and critical if I'm not.

This is the meaning of Romans 6:11—"Likewise you also, reckon yourselves to be dead indeed to sin, but alive to God in Christ Jesus our Lord" (Romans 6:11). Reckon . . . think . . . count on it . . . turn it over in your mind until you REALLY believe it . . . reckon yourself dead to sin.

Believe me: Until you have done this thing— reckoning—thinking through—the fact that you are dead to the world and alive to God . . . until you have made up your mind to that fact, you will always be irked by high Christian standards, and you'll never be completely, spontaneously happy in God's will. A dead man is the most completely *un*-bothered person you could imagine; and a resurrected person has the most overflowing joy of anyone around him. That's it: Dead . . . to sin. Alive (resurrected) . . . to God.

Discover now for yourself the basic process of human life. Living . . . is surrendering . . . to someone.

All your life before you were saved, you surrendered to self and sin. "Trespasses and sins, in which you once walked according to the course of this world, according to the prince of the power of the air, the spirit that now works in the sons of disobedience."[10]

Now your condition is changed. You are a child of God, a subject of Heaven. You have the privilege of surrendering, not to sin but to your new Sovereign and your new Friend—the Lord Jesus Christ. "And do not present your members as instruments of unrighteousness to sin, but present yourselves to God as being alive from the dead, and your members as instruments of righteousness to God."[11]

If I am truly to surrender to the Lord Jesus Christ, then the simplest way to determine right conduct will be to relate *everything* to Him.

Concerning anything questionable, ask the following:

• Will this thing honor Him, please Him, or grieve Him?

- Will it obey Him, or disobey Him?
- Is it in line with what I KNOW to be His will?
- Does it build up the kind of character and spiritual life that glorifies Him?
- Does it identify me with His followers, or with the world's crowd?
- Will it stand the test of His eyes and holiness at the judgment seat of Christ?
- Does this thing help or hinder my prayer life?
- Does this thing help or hinder my reading and study and assimilation of His Word?

Remember: "And whatever you do in word or deed, do all in the name of the Lord Jesus, giving thanks to God the Father through Him."[12]

Secondarily, your relationship with your Christian brothers and sisters is involved. Paul said: "Therefore, if food makes my brother stumble, I will never again eat meat, lest I make my brother stumble. . . . when you thus sin against the brethren, and wound their weak conscience, you sin against Christ."[13] "Rather resolve this," said the apostle, "not to put a stumbling block or a cause to fall in our brother's way."[14]

People *do* watch you, you know. What you may not realize is that *there are individuals right now who are patterning their conduct after yours.* Somebody, somewhere, is a carbon copy of you. What if he is reproducing your selfishness, your weakness, your compromise, your sin? Oh, flee now to the fountain filled with blood, and let Jesus cleanse the heart, renew the life, so that it may be the kind of example He wants it to be. "Let all things," pleads Paul, "be done for edification [building up]" (1 Cor. 14:26*b*).

The question now is not "How much may I indulge in and still be saved?" God forbid! I must rather ask, "What about Christ's will, and what about the example I set for my fellow Christians?"

This is not all, however. Your relationship to the world of the unsaved and to the demons, even to Satan himself, is involved.

Consider Satan. Is he interested in tearing down your testimony? Read Job 1 and 2 for your answer. Satan would like to lead you into sin so he could go back and laugh in the face of God and taunt Him about you! Are you going to give him that chance?

Consider the enemies of God. Read 2 Samuel 12:9-14. "By this deed," says Nathan, "you have given great occasion to the enemies of the Lord to blaspheme." Are you going to go weakly into compromise and sin and give God-hating people all around you an opportunity to blaspheme and curse God, grieving His heart afresh and reopening the wounds of Calvary? Think before you act.

You don't need any list of dos and don'ts as a Christian. All you need to keep straight is the thorough knowledge that you're born again . . . a real surrender to Christ . . . a loving concern for your fellows . . . a genuine hatred for Satan and sin . . . and a healthy fear of God. The rest is up to Him, for "He who has begun a good work in you will complete it until the day of Jesus Christ,"[15] and "it is God who works in you both to will and to do for His good pleasure" (Philippians 2:13).

COORDINATE SCRIPTURE FOR
CHAPTER 9

1. Therefore, if anyone is in Christ, he is a new creation; old things have passed away; behold, all things have become new (2 Corinthians 5:17).

2. For it was fitting for Him, for whom are all things and by whom are all things, in bringing many sons to glory, to make the author of their salvation perfect through sufferings (Hebrews 2:10).

3. You therefore must endure hardship as a good soldier of Jesus Christ (2 Timothy 2:3).

Therefore take up the whole armor of God, that

you may be able to withstand in the evil day, and having done all, to stand.

Stand therefore, having girded your waist with truth, having put on the breastplate of righteousness, and having shod your feet with the preparation of the gospel of peace; above all, taking the shield of faith with which you will be able to quench all the fiery darts of the wicked one.

And take the helmet of salvation, and the sword of the Spirit, which is the word of God; praying always with all prayer and supplication in the Spirit, being watchful to this end with all perseverance and supplication for all saints (Ephesians 6:13-18).

4. Therefore, brethren, we are debtors—not to the flesh, to live according to the flesh. For if you live according to the flesh you will die; but if by the Spirit you put to death the deeds of the body, you will live (Romans 8:12-13).

5. Likewise you also, reckon yourselves to be dead indeed to sin, but alive to God in Christ Jesus our Lord (Romans 6:11).

6. For we are His workmanship, created in Christ Jesus for good works, which God prepared beforehand that we should walk in them (Ephesians 2:10).

7. This is a faithful saying, and these things I want you to affirm constantly, that those who have believed in God should be careful to maintain good works. These things are good and profitable to men (Titus 3:8).

8. So I said, "Lord, they know that in every synagogue I imprisoned and beat those who believe on You.

And when the blood of Your martyr Stephen was shed, I also was standing by consenting to his death, and guarding the clothes of those who were killing him" (Acts 22:19-20).

9. If you were of the world, the world would love its own. Yet because you are not of the world, but I chose you out of the world, therefore the world hates you (John 15:19).

10. And you He made alive, who were dead in trespasses and sins, in which you once walked according to the course of this world, according to the prince of the power of the air, the spirit that now works in the sons of disobedience (Ephesians 2:1-2).

11. And do not present your members as instruments of unrighteousness to sin, but present yourselves to God as being alive from the dead, and your members as instruments of righteousness to God. For sin shall not have dominion over you, for you are not under law but under grace.

What then? Shall we sin because we are not under law but under grace? Certainly not!

Do you not know that to whom you present yourselves slaves to obey, you are that one's slaves whom you obey, whether of sin to death, or of obedience to righteousness?

But God be thanked that though you were slaves of sin, yet you obeyed from the heart that form of doctrine to which you were delivered. And having been set free from sin, you became the slaves of righteousness.

I speak in human terms because of the weakness of your flesh. For just as you presented your members as slaves of uncleanness, and of lawlessness leading to more lawlessness, so now present your members as slaves of righteousness for holiness. For when you were slaves of sin, you were free in regard to righteousness.

What fruit did you have then in these things of which you are now ashamed? For the end of those things is death.

But now having been set free from sin, and having become slaves of God, you have your fruit to holiness, and the end, everlasting life.

For the wages of sin is death, but the gift of God is eternal life in Jesus Christ our Lord (Romans 6:13-23).

12. And whatever you do in word or deed, do all in the name of the Lord Jesus, giving thanks to God the Father through Him (Colossians 3:17).

13. But when you thus sin against the brethren, and wound their weak conscience, you sin against Christ.

Therefore, if food makes my brother stumble, I will never again eat meat, lest I make my brother stumble (1 Corinthians 8:12-13).

14. Therefore let us not judge one another anymore, but rather resolve this, not to put a stumbling block

or a cause to fall in our brother's way (Romans 14:13).

15. Being confident of this very thing, that He who has begun a good work in you will complete it until the day of Jesus Christ (Philippians 1:6).